The Singapore Plotters

by

Donald S. Lawson

authorHOUSE™

1663 LIBERTY DRIVE, SUITE 200
BLOOMINGTON, INDIANA 47403
(800) 839-8640
WWW.AUTHORHOUSE.COM

First published by AuthorHouse 11/10/05

ISBN: 1-4208-8683-5 (e)
ISBN: 1-4208-8682-7 (sc)

Printed in the United States of America
Bloomington, Indiana

This book is printed on acid-free paper.

INTRODUCTION

How wonderful it would be if you woke up one morning and unexpectedly you came into an inheritance from a long-lost relative or a forgotten friend "It does happen," but not very often. So, if you receive notification in the mail advising you that you have come into an inheritance, which has been unclaimed for many years, **BEWARE** it could be from a "crooked Lawyer", or a "sophisticated con artist "trying to part you from your hard earned cash. You could also lose your home. You could be the target of a slick con operator... "I was taken in by one of them"

These unscrupulous scam operators, or criminals also call themselves "Inheritance Specialists or Executors"— but they didn't find me by doing research. I was simply one of the hundreds of victims across the country that is targeted in mass mailings. Hundreds of individuals with the same surname receive notification that dormant funds from long lost relatives have been located. The letter read as follows; the person has died and having left no will, you have been identified as the next of kin. Many of these recipients are lured by false reports, which supposedly explain where the inheritance is located and how it can be claimed. The con operator will also offer to process your claim for a share of this inheritance. Everyone on the mailing list receives the same information, so chances are almost zero that you are actually kin. In the rare instance when someone on the mailing list gets the right to claim the inheritance funds, the story begins to change, They may actually tell you that an amount of funds is required to cover tax, stamp duties, and legal expenses etc. You can protect yourself by checking other sources before sending funds in response to an "Inheritance claim" solicitation. Checking with relatives about recent deaths in the family is one approach.

Remember, legitimate lawyers, accountants, of wills and inheritance, who have been named to distribute inheritance funds to rightful heirs normally do not ask anyone to pay upfront fees for stamp duty etc.

This inheritance scam, is one of those letters that had being mailed to me in the United Kingdom from a person who calls himself Bhathia Keok. The contents you are about to read in this book is a true story that happen, and I feel there is a need to put this story in the public arena for people to draw their own conclusions.

Chapter 1

The Story

"This is how the Story begins". It was about 09.30 on the 15th day of April 2004. My wife Curla and I were having our early morning coffee she was reading the morning mail as she usually does. Then out of the blue she said to me "you're going to love this". I said "what" She said "manner from haven" Then she handed me a letter from the "Bank of China", written by one Bhathia .Keok.

Before I could finish reading this letter my wife interrupted me saying, "You have inherited a lot of money, nine million five hundred British pounds". "Wow". She added "that's a lot of money If it's real you could soon be a millionaire". I did not comment but continued reading the letter just to be sure she was not winding me up, she was not. I was very surprised as I was not aware of any rich distant relative. I was tempted to bin the letter but that amount of money overwhelmed me.

It's like winning the national lottery it could change my life forever and others too. So where do I go from here I said? "Well, if I'm right—and feeling like how most people would, I could go in two directions – (1) if I do nothing, I could bin the letter, or (2) take a chance and contact the writer. "There you have it". I did not need much encouragement to contact the writer. So I did so in the following manner by phone and letter.

In my madness I did not pay attention to simple details like the phone number 00+8821 646655522, this was a satellite number, the "Bank of China Singapore Branch", would not be using a satellite number for commercial contact with the public. This was confirmed when I finally contacted the bank towards the end of the journey.

Attn Donald Lawson
Harvey House Green
Breatford
Middlesex
TW8 0DH
United Kingdom

April 7, 2004

My name is Bhathia Keok , and work fir the Bank of China !J2 Singapore. T am the **head** of interval audit department. While we wore conducting the audit system check fpr last year, I came across investment accounts that have been dormant for many years, All accounts be1dnq to the same person and the monies total about 9,000,00-Nine Million British Pounds. The reason why r am contacting you nor is because, the funds hare been lying dormant

for almost 25 years and your last name and country of origin is similar to that of the late Investor. Due to the short time frame we have on this I have asked a colleague of nine coming to the UK to deliver this letter to you
Banking regulation requires me to notify our regulatory bodies whom making our yearly returns about this dormant accounts once they have been dormant for.25,rears. The 25 years on these accounts should become due at the end of April so It is essential that we move quickly.
The account holder was British and after expensive enquiries by me r discovered that Mr. Lawson who migrated to Hong Kong In May of 1967 died In Indonesia I'n October 1988. We have made extensive enquiries to find a next of kin without any success. This explains why the funds hove remained dormant far almost twenty-five years. This is where I your help, I am 1n a Position to put together all the necessary documentation .o. which will be required to transfer the funds to an account which will be nominated by you. By this I mean that, the rights and privileges bestowed on the Investor will be transferred to you I have the co-operation of a Judge who Is willing to prepare the legal papers to cover this.
Please be aware that by agreeing to this you will mat be at any risk all the risk is borne on my side. Also because of the shortness of time, we need to move as quickly as possible .,1 have already .invested a considerable amount of time and money in t4hs endeavor be-cause of the rewards I expect to reap upon successful completion. For confidential reasons you can call, me on 00+8821646655522, which is my Son,'s number or fax me 00+6564151448 your contact information so that we can discuss in further detail. Please because of the mature of' the transaction It is Important that we keep this between us.

Regards,

Bhathia Keok

BK ORIGIANL BANK LETTER

Translation Letter. 1

My name is Bahathia Keok and I work for the Bank of China in Singapore. I am the head of internal audit department. While we were conducting the audit system check for the last year I came across investments accounts that have been dormant for many years. All accounts belong to the same person and the monies total about 9,000,000 — Nine Million British Pounds. The reason why I am contacting you now is because the funds have been lying dormant for almost 25 years and your last name and country of origin is similar to that of the late investor. Due to the short time frame we have on this I have asked a colleague of mine coming to the UK to deliver this letter to you. Banking regulation requires me to notify our regulatory bodies when making our yearly returns about these dormant accounts once they have been dormant for 25 years. The 25 years of these accounts should become due at the end of April so it is essential that we move quickly.

The account holder was British and after expensive enquiries by me I discovered that Mr. Lawson who migrated to Hong Kong in May of 1967 and died in Indonesia in October 1988 we have extensive enquires made to find a next of kin without any success. This explains why the funds have remained dormant for almost twenty-five years. This is where I need your help.

I am in the position to put together all the necessary documentation, which will be required to transfer the funds to an account, which will be nominated by you. By this I mean that the rights and privileges bestowed on the investor will be transferred to you. I have the co-operation of a Judge who is willing to prepare the legal papers to cover this. Please be aware that by agreeing to this you will not be at any risk all the risk is borne on my side. Also because of the shortness of time we need to move quickly as possibly.

I have already invested a considerable amount of time and money in this endeavour because of the rewards I expect to reap upon successful completion. For confidential reasons you can call me on 00+8821646655522, which is my son's number, or fax me your contact information on 00+6564151446, so that we can discuss in further detail. Please because of the nature of the transaction it is important that you keep this between us Regards Bhathia Keok

Response: Letter one

After reading Bhathia Keok's letter I did not respond for several days then I finally telephoned the number. The voice at the other end answered the phone "Hello Bhathia Here" I introduced myself as the recipient, he said "good I see you have got my letter" I said "yes that's why I am calling you". His response was, "you are a lucky man Mr. Lawson" He was very polite and friendly. During the conversation that followed he explained the full contents of the letter and insisted that it must remain confidential for security reasons.

I told him that I understood and that I would be sending him a facsimile to confirm my co-operation. He told me that his spoken English was not very good, but luckily his son writes well. He then instructed me that all fax communication should be sent to his son in Singapore. Even at this early stage the plot was staring me in the face, yet there was no conscious scepticism of my objective in my mind. By that I mean there was no little amber light at the back of my mind warning of the danger, or asking the question why I should not communicate with the subject who wrote to me as the auditor who claimed he work's for the Bank of China Singapore Branch.

I was too engrossed in a state of over powering madness to get the Inheritance money. Without any further delay I sent Bhathia the fax letter simple saying Thank you for your letter dated April 2, 2004, received April 15, 2004, contents of which have been carefully noted. Whilst I am interested and would be prepared to proceed with the contents of your letter, I need to have more detailed information at your earliest. I did not have to wait very long for his response. It came the very next day in precise detail in the following format in letter 2

BK Letter: two

From the Desk of: Bhathia Keok. Attention: Mr. Lawson it was good to talk to you yesterday, I wish to thank you for your willingness to co-operate and assist me in this transaction. My spoken English as I said earlier is not very good, but luckily, my son writes well. While I was working in our private banking division, the subject came to engage in business discussion. I was the officer assigned to this case I made numerous Suggestions in line with my duties, especially giving the volume of money he wants to put in the bank. I met him on numerous occasions prior to any investments being placed. I encouraged him to consider various investment possibilities with prime ratings.

My favoured approach is to start on traditional data on blue chip, stocks and bonds. based on my advice then, we spun the money around various opportunities and made attractive margins. These margins were not the full investment potential but he desired low risk with guaranteed return on the investment. If you are familiar with private banking affairs, those who use our services usually prefer anonymity and also some level of detachment from conventional processes. In as bio data form he listed no next of kin. In the field of private banking opening an account with us no one will know of its existence. Accounts are rarely held under a name, depositors use numbers and codes to make their accounts anonymous.

Because of my personal dealings with him, when I was transferred to the audit department and there was no inactivity on his account, I was able to realize the opportunity that was presenting itself. I will initiate the process with my high court judge friend once I got a copy of our identity; either your passport copy or driver's license or birth certificate the judge has confirmed that the indemnity transfer of rights and privileges will be ready in two or three days from the moment he receives your identity. This confers on you the beneficiary rights in relation to the investment. Once I get the legal document I will take it over to the probate office and apply for a letter of administration. The probate office will then contact banks to furnish them with balances on this account where applicable. This final balance is what we will put in your application. The application will then be place on the notice board for 48 hours. This is to enable any member of the public who has a quarry against the application to do so. Once this is done successfully, we will be issued a letter of administration for the bank my bank to transfer the funds via our corresponding bank in Europe.

This whole process will be accomplished within 10 working days. Remember that you are to split the money 50/50 for my services. Please confirm that in writing that you are in agreement with this split. Also take note that the ratio should be adhered to strictly, there is enough for both of us. On completion of this transaction you will be required to hold the funds in your account until I come over to your country for the sharing of the money. All modalities for the successful completion of this transaction has been mapped out provided you maintain absolute confidentiality and keep with the instructions that I hand over to you from time to time religiously. I will be travelling to Hong Kong, where I will begin the process with the high court judge. So please send me a copy of your identification through to my confidential fax number in Hong Kong 0085230013409. You can always talk to me by phone via 0088-21646655522 I await for your response as soon as possible, Best regards Bhathia Keok.

It did not take me long to respond positively to the subject request for my identification. Even at this stage, my madness had disappeared and euphoria set in. I could see the changes in my life and things I wanted to do for others. All my dreams could become a reality. The contents have been carefully noted. I do confirm that upon the completion of the application and transfer of the final balance of the funds you will receive Fifty (50%) Percent from the amount received for your services. Please note that by accepting the Rights and Privileges as the next of kin these will be accepted as legal documentation for transferring to me.

Although you said that you are the head of the audit department for the Bank of China in Singapore. I would like to receive from you some documentation of your identity and confirmation from the bank as to whom I am dealing with, Passport details etc by fax, will be accepted to be followed by hard copy by normal mail or courier. I will also need your private address to which all communication can be forwarded for security purposes and legitimacy.

Please let me have these documents as soon as possible. I am sure you are aware that with the world situation and threat of terrorist activities in Europe and around the world, all banks have a duty to advise the relevant authorities about the origin and transfer of any large amount of funds being transmitted or received .As soon as I received my request from you, my passport details will be forwarded to you by fax for the Judge to prepare the documents for the transfer of the Rights and Privileges of the late Mr. Lawson to me I wait to hear from you at your earliest. Donald

Then on April 19th 2004 I received part of my request from the subject, with his home address >> Flat A, 2F Knight Garden, 11-12 Tak Hing Street, Jordan, Kawloan, Hong Kong, also attached, was his Passport details. In the same communication he confirmed receiving my fax details and that he would be going to see the Judge later the following day. I will be sending you another fax tomorrow April 20, 2004 to explain the timing of things. Please also find included in my fax all the information you requested "I look forward to the beginning of a mutually benefiting relationship". Best Regards Bhathia

Donald S. Lawson

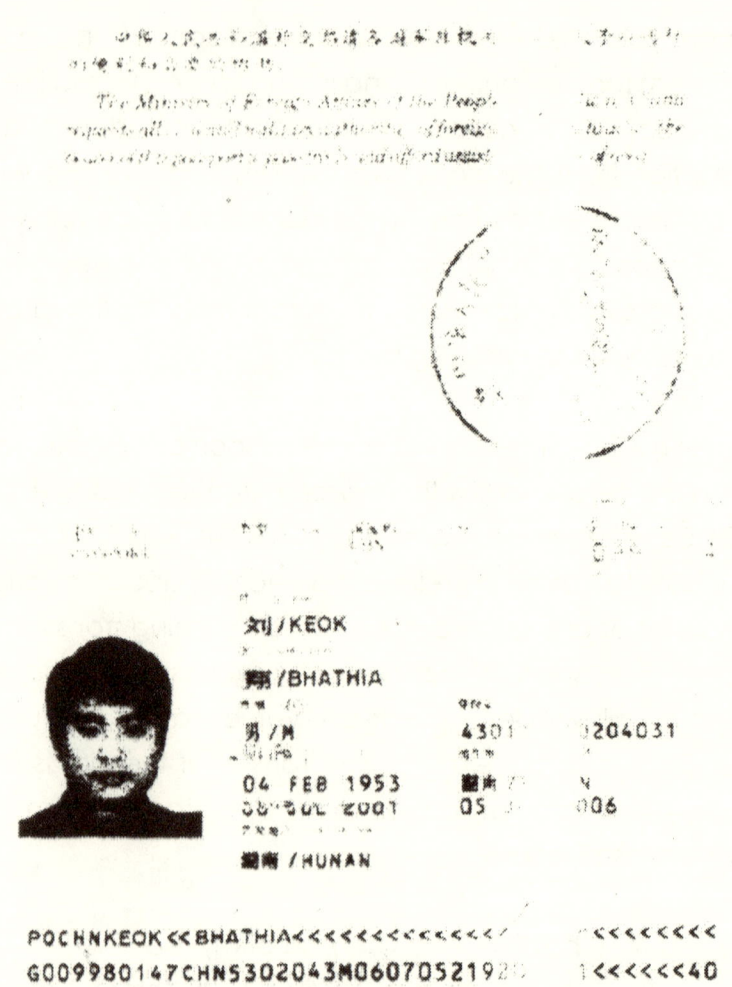

Passport details

Chapter 2

Rights & Privileges

Several days after the subject had received my passport details he confirm to me that he had seen the judge the very next day as planned and that he checked my identity to confirm that my surname Lawson is the same as the deceased investor. The reason I asked for your identity he said, was because the judge who is a long term friend was not willing to go ahead without confirming from your identity that the surname are the same. He then when on to tell me that the Judge will be initiating the process from today April 19-4-04 and that he is hoping that by Friday 24-4-04 at the latest he should be in a position to issue the indemnity transfer of rights and privileges. This legal document will transfer the rights as regards to the investment to Donald Lawson. As things stand, he said he should be able to apply for a letter of administration at the "Probate Office in Hong Kong by Friday or Monday latest the following week." This will all depend on when the transfer of rights is issued. The transfer of rights is the reason why we are in this position to apply for the letter of administration.

He then went on to tell me in a very friendly manner, "Donald, I will be away from this evening and I will not be back till Thursday evening 03-05.-04 your time London. I will then be in a position to give you further updates immediately I get back. The important thing is once the judge issues the transfer of rights that becomes the basis for you being the "next of kin". I look forward to confirming this to you on Friday.04_05_04 Best Regards Bhathia.

The expected confirmation from the subject did not arrive on the date promised until two days later Monday 06-05 –04 the communication arrived in the usual manner:

From the Desk of Bhathia Keok

How are you and the family? I am sorry I could not send you an update yesterday. I got back late last night. I have today been to see the judge and he informed me that he has issued the transfer of right and privileges in your name and has submitted it to the probate section. On Monday I will go over to the probate office and apply for a letter of administration. What should then happen is that the probate office will write to all banks asking for any name or account match, this is so to enable us to have a final figure to put on the application.

Once this figure is confirmed, our application will be placed on the notice board for 48 hours. The Idea behind this is to enable any member of the public who has a query against our application to do so. This is one aspect that worries because I have no control over what might happen. (That is I have no way of stopping any member of the public from issuing a query against our application) My only consolation is that the claim has remained unclaimed for so long, consequently I am of the opinion that it is unlikely that there will be a query from any member of the public. Once the outcome is favourably it will be plain sailing till the conclusion.

I will also go the inland revenue to get the tax assessment this is to enable me to get the tax burden so that I can pay it and by so doing acquire the tax certificate which is paramount especially as we are transferring the funds out of my country The tax has to be paid for three reasons. (1) The length of time it has taken for the claim to be made (2) You are a foreigner and I do not want to focus any attention to the transaction because my tax authority takes a very dim view on tax evasion (3) Before the funds are transferred the tax will definitely become an issue I don't want that happening. have applied for a loan on the remaining equity on my house. This will take care of the tax payment. Do not concern yourself with this I will take care of it financially. The reason why I mentioned it, is because I want you to appreciate that I am putting in both my time and my financial resources to make this transaction successful. It is so easy for you not to appreciate because you are so far removed from everything I am doing.

I have thought this transaction through and will keep you informed as to the timing and outcome, the moment I hear it. Please give me a call to confirm your understanding of the situation. I look forward to hearing from you .Best regards Bhatia

May 4. 04 "From the desk of Bhatia Keok". How are you and the family, well I hope. I am sorry I could not send the fax as promised yesterday. This was because I had a problem with my machine. As mentioned last Friday, I heard the good news. I cannot describe the joy I felt on hearing the news because it was mixed with a great feeling of relief. The relief comes from knowing that under the present circumstances, we are now well placed to conclude the transaction successfully. To best describe how I felt at that moment, I have to compare it to the feeling a woman who has had multiple miscarriages gets when she finally carries a pregnancy to its full term.

The last two days have been very stressful, because I had no way of determining the outcome. Thankfully all that is now behind us, as things stand at the moment. I have been made to understand that because you are a foreigner and the transaction involves funds over $1,000,000, you will be invited to come to Singapore to sign for the release of the funds as well as the documents. The probate office has issued the letter of administration. This was transferred in your file to the Singapore Claim Board. It is the claim board who will invite you to come and sign for the release.

All the documents in relation to the transaction will then be sent to your home address by registered mail. The documents will be needed by you to explain the source of the funds once the money is in your Bank. Because of the present world climate, we need to be able to explain its source.

I do hope your work commitment will not prevent you from being available to sign for the release that would be disastrous from the point of view of completing the transaction. I have also received the tax assessment. Our tax burden comes to approximately $220,000. I was able to secure a loan of

$185,000 because that was the only equity left on my house. With the good news from the Probate I made the part payment yesterday. So that the evidence of tax payment also enable them to transfer the file to the board. I am making arrangements to secure the balance of $35,000 through a close friend in China. I should be able to get it by next week Wednesday so as to enable us acquire the tax certificate. Do not concern yourself with this. I will take Care of it.

According to my investigation, the final approval will come from "Singapore Claim Board" since the funds are in Singapore. This is because the SDC has the final say. This is just a Beaucratic process because all the documents apart from the fax are already in place.

They will be contacting you by post or fax to inform you of the final approval and the date to come to sign for release of the funds and document. Please let me know the moment you hear from them because as things stand I will be remaining in the background. This is to avoid eyebrows being raised in relation to the claim. I will make the tax payment next week so as to enable us to get the tax clearance certificate before the final transfer,

to prevent them stopping the transfer at the final stage. If you require any help with investing your share, do not hesitate to ask me for advice. I will be only too happy to assist you in that direction. Any information with regards to the transaction,will be known to you. Keep me informed immediately you hear anything. All we can do now is wait for a date for you to sign for the release. Best regards Bhathia.

I was now in a state of melancholy to say the least, but I had to calm myself down enough to write to Bhathia Keok, thanking him for his phone and fax communication of May 4th. 2004. I told him I could understand how he felt when he received the good news last Friday. I could hear the excitement in your voice I said. I too was joyful on receiving the positive outcome of your endeavours. Please put your mind at rest and be assured that I will keep you informed as and when I hear from the "Claim Board". I note from your communication, that as a foreigner and the amount being in excess of $1,000 000, I will be invited to come to Singapore to sign the release of the funds as well as the legal documents. I would like to suggest that the claim board send the hard copy documents to me by courier at my London address. I will then swear an affidavit as well as my passport details and return them by courier to the "Singapore Claim Board"

The reason why I am reluctant to travel to Singapore is that I recently had a major operation from which I have not fully recovered. I will put this request to the claim board when I hear from them. Regarding the last paragraph of your letter, what does SDC mean? I do understand the rest of the paragraph and I carefully noted the contents. I will therefore inform you the moment I hear from the "Singapore Claim Board".

Chapter 3

The Claim Board

SINGAPORE CLAIMS BOARD

Fax: +6568279062

FAX

TO: Donald Lawson	FROM: Andrew Chuang
FAX: +442085687905	DATE: 19/05/04
PHONE:	NO. OF PAGES: 1
RE: Claim	OUR REFERENCE: AH175482

☐ PLEASE REPLY ☒ FOR YOUR INFORMATION ☐ PLEASE COMMENT ☐ URGENT

This is to inform you that we have started processing your above referenced claim.

As part of this process, you must attend an interview. Said interview has been scheduled for you at our offices here in Singapore for Friday, 28 May 2004 at 10:30am.

Also, we must receive evidence of your completed tax payments before said interview.

Please fax the following documents to us, failure to do so may result in your interview being postponed, and your claim denied:
> Passport
> Certified IMR Form
> Completed DC2 Form

Please quote the above reference number on any communication.

Claim Board File Letter

Thursday, May 20-04" It was on this day that I received a fax claim letter from Andrew Chuang of the Singapore Claim

Donald S. Lawson

Board Reference: AH175482 advising that they have started processing the reference inheritance claim and that as part of the process I must attend an interview in Singapore. The said interview was scheduled for me at their offices in Singapore on the May 25-04 at 10.30 AM. It was at this time that I noticed that there was no address, nor covering letter with the fax communication I began to feel uncomfortable, nevertheless I thought I would acknowledge the fax letter dated May 19-04 regarding the referenced claim.

I immediately responded telling the writer that I had received his fax letter, and that I would be contacting him again shortly, with regard to his request for documentation to the claim. I told him that I would be grateful if he could send me the Singapore Claim Board's mailing address and telephone number that were missing from his communication to me. I finish the text by saying that I would be forwarding the documents by fax and hard copy to him shortly. Several times, I tried to contact the writer Andrew Chuang from the number on the fax without success. "Needless to say I was very disappointed so I informed Bhathia Keok of the developing problems, so as to avoid further delays; I sent my response, to him for delivery to the Singapore Claim Board. Here is the response.

Hello Bhathia, I have today, May 20-04 received from the Singapore Claim Board a fax advising me that they have started processing the claim. They said that as part of this process I must attend an interview. The interview, scheduled for me at their offices in Singapore on Friday May 28-04 at 10.30 A.M. They indicated that they needed to receive evidence of the completed tax payments before the interview. They also want me to fax them the following documents: - Passport,

Certified IMR Form, and Completed DC2 form. Failure to do so may result in my interview being postponed, and the claim denied. Apart from the passport details, you will have to advise me regarding these forms. Your assistance will also be required and appreciated if you could forward all feature communication to Mr. Chuang of the. Singapore Claim Board as I am unable to make contact, the address is also missing.

May 21-04 From the desk of Bhathia Keok,

Hello my friend Donald Sequel to your last fax regarding the final conclusion of our transaction, I wish to furthermore explain how we should go about the transaction in order to guarantee success at the end of it all.

In the fax that was sent to you by the Claim Board, you were required to come down to Singapore for an interview before the funds will be finally transferred to your account, but after much deliberation, I feel that it will not be in our best interest for you to come down for such interview which may take anything between 30 minutes to 2 hours, the problem with such interview is that we have no way of determining in what direction it will take (by that I mean how do we know what question they will ask).

This whole transactions is based on my ability to provide all the documentation required for the transaction to be successfully concluded. I have been able to provide all that but I did not anticipate that they would call you for an interview, it is too risky for all concerned, I have therefore made discrete

Donald S. Lawson

enquiries if there is another option we could take in order to avoid you coming down to Singapore .

As things stand I understand that what you need to do is send a fax stating that due to medical advise you are unable to make long haul flight and would like to use either option A or option B depending on which option you prefer, Is it possible for you to get medical cover this? I will try to go through the options giving you the advantages and disadvantages of each of the options because you have to make the choice as to which option you are comfortable with.

I have been reliable informed that the claim board can appoint one of their accredited attorneys to represent you if the request is made by you. The advantage of option A is that you do not have to attend the interview because the lawyer handles the process for you. (2) The fact that the lawyer is one of their accredited attorneys means that he would know how to handle the transaction on our behalf. The disadvantage is that it would take longer to close the transaction as long as two more weeks (2) We will need to give them as much as 5% of our money for their fees, this by implication reduces what he both get. Option B entails you requesting to use their European payment centre in swissland. The advantage of this is that the transaction can also be closed in one day and I understand the process all things being equal will only be based on confirmed verification (2) It will not cost you any thing apart from your hotel and transport cost.

I have been reliable informed that the claim board can appoint one of their accredited attorneys to represent you if the request is made by you. The advantage of option A is that you do not have to attend the interview because the lawyer handles the process for you. (2) The fact that the lawyer is one of their accredited attorneys means that he would know how to handle the transaction on our behalf. The disadvantage is that it would take longer to close the transaction as long as two more weeks (2) We will need to give them as much as 5% of our money for their fees, this by implication reduces what he both get. Option B entails you requesting to use their European payment centre in Swissland. The advantage of this is that the transaction can also be closed in one day and I understand the process all things being equal will only be based on confirmed verification (2) It will not cost you any thing apart from your hotel and transport cost.

The advantage is that you still have to meet somebody although it will be only one individual (2) We do have any control of how the meeting will go. You have to chose your preferred option. As far as the documents are concerned, I am still trying to raise the balance of the taxes for us to get the Tax Clearance Certificate, But I am already having high hopes of getting the balance soonest through a financer friend of mine. You can also state in the letter that a copy of the Certificate will be sent to them. All the other documents which was requested Certified IMR form,DC2 Form etc, are all contained in your claim file and that they should refer to the Probate Office for verification. In summary write the letter as early mentioned with regards medical advice then request for either their accredited lawyers or to go to the European center. Please let me know what you decide, Best regards Bhathia.

Donald S. Lawson

The very next day i respond to the subject fax sequel, I inform him that I would go for option A which meant that I would not have to attend the interview because an appointed lawyer could handle the whole process on my behalf. I also advised him to send this fax communication verb age to Andrew. Chuang of the. Singapore Claim Board:

Hello Mr. Chuang further to my fax letter of May 20- 04, I am responding further to your fax dated May 19-04 regarding the reference inheritance claim. You mention that as part of the process I must attend an interview at you offices in Singapore on Friday May 28-04 at 10.30 AM. Unfortunately, as things stand I am unable to make long haul flights of any kind due to a chronic back pain, which would make the Journey extremely painful and uncomfortable. I enclosed a letter from my medical practitioner. Under these circumstances, I would respectfully request that the claim board appoint one of their accredited lawyers to represent and handle the process on my behalf. Regarding the completed tax payment the Tax Clearance Certificate I understand will be sent to you shortly. All the other documents that were requested: Certified IMR form and DC2 form etc are all contained in the claim file bundle I am told by Bathia. >>>

I wrote on June 7-04: With reference to the project letter dated April 2-04 I am getting a little concerned with the results to date from the Singapore Claim Board and yourself. I am being kept in the dark, as I do not have any evidence or copies of any documents that you have filed on my behalf in Hong Kong and Singapore regarding the project. As a professional person, you know the value of doing things the right way. Since I received your first letter dated April 2.-04 and the subsequent faxes, and voice communication I have no reason to doubt what you have written to me. I also believe that all the rights and privileges were transferred to me as the next of kin after the 48-hour period. However, I thought you would have sent me some evidence of that fact. I believe that this is a vital aspect of the whole situation.

When I finally received a fax from the Singapore Claim Board, I was also very disappointed, that although I responded to them advising a Mr. Andrew Chuang that I received his fax I have not being able to make any further contact to that communication number. Furthermore, I sent a letter to them via you with my Passport details and official Medical Documents, requesting that they appoint an accredited Lawyer to act on my behalf.

I did expect some acknowledgement of my communication. This did not arrive, nor did I receive any communication from the appointed Lawyer who would be acting on my behalf. "I do find this a little strange" I hope you can understand why I am so disappointed how currently things are. My telephone bill is getting bigger and bigger the Telephone Provider today. The telephone calls that I have been making to you on this number, 00+8821646655522 (Inmarsat) is a satellite phone. The calls are £4.00 per minute a total of £725.82 to date. You mention that this matter must remain confidential; if there is nothing to hide; I wondered if you could use a landline, which is more economical The telefax no: 0085230103409 is also far more economical than voice mail for communication purposes. It is probably as expensive for you to communicate with me as it is for me to communicate with you. At least I am using a landline. Please send me a fax before Monday 31

May 2004 and let me know how the program is progressing by the Singapore Claim Board, as I have not heard from them to date.

It was several days before the subject communicated with the following:> I was very unhappy he said when I received your fax dated 12ᵗʰ. of June 2004. Two things became clear to me. (1) whatever the incident which you said you will discuss with me when we meet, is definitely affecting your judgement and how you see life in general and I think it is most unfair from my own perspective.

(2) I also think that you have not only not been understanding my faxes, but you have not been hearing anything I have been saying to you. I have never at any point kept you in the dark, I have told you over and over again at what point everything will be given to you. I do not think you really appreciate what I have done so far. I cannot also be blamed for whatever transpired between your goodself and Mr Chuang I have no control over that. I have told you that when they contact you, then you need to find out what the problem is. I have also told you that you have been approved, the use of a lawyer. This does not in any way mean that a lawyer has been appointed for you. A Lawyer still needs to be appointed for you.

Whatever your complaints with them are, take it up with them when they contact you, As I said earlier, the two factors which I observed earlier are affecting your judgement. I Also think that you are not a patient man. I think you have to learn to be patient, What would you have done if you had invested your life savings in this transaction as I have done. I told you I will be away until Monday, but yet my son told me you called and also you sent your last fax could you not wait for me to get back. We are at the final stage, Yes we have been here for a long time now, my future depends on the successful conclusion so I can not afford to have negative thoughts. Your future Is definitely not depended on its conclusion so you can afford to have them, In the meantime I will try and find what is causing the delay at the Singapore Claim Board. Best regards Bhathia Keok.

Chapter: 4

Foreign Operations Department

It was several days when I received a telephone call from Bhathia Keok explaining to me that he is reliably informed that Mr. Chuang of the. Singapore Claim Board was away for short break and that I would hear from them soon. Then on June 25.2004 a fax communication arrived from the FOREIGN OPERATIONS DEPARTMENT in Singapore the writer a Mr. Albert Jagger, the text contained a new Claim Reference No.2784158/04. I acknowledge the Fax communisation in the normal way.

水切船空
FOREIGN OPERATIONS DEPARTMENT
EAST COAST ROAD SINGAPORE 428898
Telephone: 62905507 Facsimile: 64151446

25 June 2004

Attention: Donald Lawson
BY FAX

Re: Claim Ref. No. 2784158/04

Dear Sir:

Your file has been forwarded to us for further processing to determine your entitlement, and a new claim number has been assigned to you, please quote it in any communication with us.

You have been cleared for legal representation, you will be notified once you have been assigned an accredited attorney.

Please call me if you have any question.

Yours faithfully,

Albert Jaggers

FOREIGN OPERATIONS DEPARTMENT
FAX TEXT ONE (1)

Foreign Operations Department

Hello Mr. Jagger, further to my fax of June 25th 04,

I am responding further regarding the reference inheritance claim. You mention that as part of the process I must attend an interview at you offices in Singapore Unfortunately as things stand at the moment I am unable to make long haul flights of any kind due to a chronic back pain which would

Donald S. Lawson

make the journey extremely painful and uncomfortable. I enclosed a letter from my medical practitioner. Under these circumstances I would respectfully request that you appoint one of your accredited lawyers to represent and handle the process on my behalf.

I also wish to bring to your attention that this information including the completed tax payment the Tax Clearance Certificate plus the other documents which were requested, Certified IMR form and DC2 form etc are all contained in the claim file bundle according to Bhatia keok the completed tax payment the Tax Clearance Certificate plus the other documents which were requested, Certified IMR form and DC2 form etc are all contained in the claim file bundle according to Bhatia keok.

At this stage of operations I was getting very mixed signals in my head that something was not going as it should never the less, I informed Bhatia keok of developments. Then on July 12-04, I received this fax communication from Albert Jaggers of the so called Foreign Operations Department advising that because I am unable to personally attend the hearing the law requires that for your own protection I must be represented at the said hearing by an Accredited Board Certified Solicitor/ Practitioner. Please contact:

承塑懒惫
FOREIGN OPERATIONS DEPARTMENT
EAST COAST ROAD SINGAPORE 428898
Telephone: 62995507 Facsimile 64151446

12 July 2004

Attention: Donald Lawson
BY FAX

Re: Claim Ref. No. 2784158/04

Dear Sir:

As you are unable to personally attend your hearing, the law requires that for your own protection, you must be represented at said hearing by an Accredited Board Certified Solicitor/ Practitioner.

Please contact:
Lee Associate BVBA
3 Temesk Ave
16-03 Centinnel Towers
Singapore 039198
Tel: 65 62 960725

Yours faithfully,

Albert Jaggers

Foreign Operations Department
FOB FAX TEXT 2

Several days after hearing from Jaggers I wrote to him saying "Thank you for your fax letter of Monday July 12, 2004, regarding the hearing for my claim entitlement and for introducing an Accredited Board Certified Solicitor /Practitioner to represent me at the said hearing. Although you have sent me the name of the firm, and telephone number, you have not sent me a contact name, and the telephone number is unobtainable. It

Donald S. Lawson

would be most helpful if you could send me a contact name"
and the correct telephone number". Then on the following
day July 13, 2004 I received another fax with a contact name
and the correct telephone number. The very next day I
telephoned the Singapore number, that was answered with
a voicemail saying "Law Offices, If you wish to speak to a
legal practitioner, press 1, or if you wish to send a fax press 2.
I pressed 1 and a voice came on the phone, and repeated
"Law Offices".

I introduced myself and asked for the contact name. The
person said the contact, Miss Elias was in court but they would
get her to call me. The contact called me at around 4 pm
(which would be very late night in Singapore) and introduced
herself as Miss Ellis Elias. She told me that she is the *accredited
lawyer* appointed by the Foreign Operations Department to
handle my claim entitlement. She went on to say that she
was going to the Foreign Operations Department to look at
the file the next day and would phone and also send a fax
after seeing the file. I then received the fax. Throughout this
process I was keeping Bhatia informed of the proceedings

LEE ASSOCIATES BVBA

The Solicitor
Lee Associates BVBA

To: Mr. Donald Lawson

Re: Representation Claim Reference No. 2784158/04

Dear Sir

Per our earlier conversation, and based on the information I received from the FOD, your total expected inheritance payout is € 13,526,000 Thirteen Million Five Hundred and Twenty Six Thousand Euros.

I have asked that our interview be rescheduled. I have a tentative date of Friday, 23 July 2004 at 2.30pm which will be confirmed as soon as the FOD receives affirmation that you have retained my firm to represent you. Said affirmation will be in the form of a notice of representation.

In order for me to view your file and/or request specific information pertaining to your claim, I will need you to sign and fax me the following Power of Attorney and the last page of this letter as confirmation that you have retained us to represent you.

Below is the list of documents I will need to effectively represent you before the FOD. Once I receive the signed

Donald S. Lawson

Power of Attorney, I will confirm with the FOD which, if any of the required documents are still outstanding.

Passport
Letter of Probate
Original Investment Certificate
Tax Clearance Certificate
Our Fees for representing you in this matter will be €9,000.00 Nine Thousand Euros, payable upon conclusion. However, a retainer of €16,000 Sixteen Euros will be required to cover expenses. See breakdown below.

Registration Fee -   €1.500.00
IMR   € 500.00
Certification/Affirmation of Documents - €475.00
Stamp Duty   € 13.526

The registration will validate your claim so that in the unlikely event of any dispute, you will be primary claimant. Also all the documents you submitted have to be certified as true copies. The FOD will not accept them without certification as rue copies. The IMR form is the application for payment, which also has to be certified.

Please sign and fax back to my attention the Power of Attorney and this page, along with confirmation of payment of the retainer, so that I can file a notice of Representation with the FOD.

Please see addendum on how to pay your retainer.

LEE ASSOCIATES BVBA

14 July 2004

TO: Mr. Donald Lawson

Re: Representation Claim Reference No. 2784158/04

Dear Sir,

Per our earlier conversation, and based on the information I received from the FOD, your total expected inheritance payout is € 13,526,000 Thirteen Million Five Hundred and Twenty Six Thousand Euros.

I have asked that your interview be rescheduled, I have a tentative date of Friday, 23 July 2004 at 2:30pm which will be confirmed as soon as the FOD receives affirmation that you have retained my firm to represent you, said affirmation will be in the form of a notice of representation.

In order for me to view your file and/or request specific information pertaining to your claim, I will need you to sign and fax me the following Power of Attorney and the last page of this letter as confirmation that you have retained us to represent you.

Below is the list of documents I will need to effectively represent you before the FOD. Once I receive the signed power of attorney, I will confirm with the FOD which if any of the required documents are still outstanding.

3 TEMASEK AVENUE, 06-03 CENTENNIAL TOWER, SINGAPORE 039190
TELEPHONE/ FAX: 65 63960725

LEE ASSOCIATES BVBA
TEXT 1

Donald S. Lawson

LEE ASSOCIATES BVBA

Passport
Letter of Probate
Original Investment Certificate
Tax Clearance Certificate

Our fees for representing you in this matter will be C9,000.00
Nine Thousand Euros payable upon conclusion. However, a retainer
of €16,000 Sixteen Thousand Euros will be required to cover
expenses, see breakdown below.

Registration Fee - €1,500.00
IMR Form - €500
Certification/Affirmation of Documents- €475
Stamp Duty - C13,526

The registration will validate your claim, so that in the unlikely event
of any dispute, you will be primary claimant. Also, all the documents
you submitted have to be certified as true copies, the FOD will not
accept them without certification. The IMR form is the application for
payment, which also has to be certified.

Please sign and fax back to my attention the Power of Attorney and
this page, along with confirmation of payment of the retainer, so
that I can file a notice of Representation with the FOD.

Please see addendum on how to pay your retainer.

Yours faithfully,

Michelle Elias

Michelle C. Elias
Senior Associate

ACCEPTED & AGREED TO:

....
CLIENT NAME: **DONALD LAWSON**

3 TEMASEK AVENUE, 06-03 CENTENNIAL TOWER, SINGAPORE 039190
TELEPHONE/ FAX: 65 63960725

LEE ASSOCIATES BVBA
Text 2

LEE ASSOCIATES BVBA

REPUBLIC OF SINGAPORE

SPECIAL POWER OF ATTORNEY

I/We .... DONALD LAWSON .... ON THIS THE ...... 14TH ... OF ... JULY ...... ,
2004 .

DO HEREBY GRANT A SPECIAL POWER OF ATTORNEY TO:

LEE ASSOCIATES BVBA
3 Temasek Avenue
06-03 Centennial Tower
Singapore 039190

FOR REPRESENTATION IN THE MATTER OF .... INHERITANCE ~ SEE
FOR CLAIM REFERENCE NUMBER 2784158/04 ....

....

....

TO FINAL DETERMINATION THEREOF.

SIGNATURE ....

DATE ....

WITNESS SIGNATURE ....

FULL NAME ....

DATE ....

---

3 TEMASEK AVENUE, 06-03 CENTENNIAL TOWER, SINGAPORE 039190
TELEPHONE/ FAX: 05 63960725

LEE ASSOCIATES BVBA
Text 3

Donald S. Lawson

Chapter:5

The Pressure

July 15- 2004 Lee Associates BVBA, 3 Temasek Avenue,06-03 Centennial Tower, Singapore 093190, Michelle C Elias, FOD: Claim Reference. No 2784158/04

Miss Elias, Thank you for your fax letter dated July 14, 2004 regarding my above referenced Inheritance Claim.

I note that you have a tentative interview date for Friday 23rd July 2004 at 2.30 pm, to be confirmed as soon as the Foreign Operations Department (FOB)receives affirmation, that you have been retained to represent me in the above mentioned claim. I therefore enclose page three of your fax communication duly signed and witnessed as confirmation of your appointment together with passport details. All other documents are with the FOB. Regarding your retainer, I am not yet in a position to forward the expenses requested, and wondered if a mutually acceptable arrangement can be reached with your firm. I suggest that a nominal sum of €2000 Euros on account, be paid now and the full balance of fees and expenses as soon as the transaction is processed and completed plus five (5%) percent of the total amount due will be paid to your firm for the service provided.

This is the way; I'm told that most solicitors/Attorneys work. I trust that this proposal is acceptable to you and look forward to hearing from you by return. Finally, your bank co-ordinates are unclear and cannot be read. Please send a fresh copy. Also I will need to have hard copies of all future documents. Sincerely Donald Needless to say Michelle C Elias was not prepared to accept my proposal. She was adamant that The retainer of €16.000 sixteen Thousand Euros be paid upfront into a bank account in Belgium. In view of the activities with the this Lawyer, Bhathia Keok was no longer sending me fax messages. He was now phoning me daily pressuring me to pay €16.000 Sixteen Thousand Euros to Michelle C Elias the solicitor.

During one of Bhathia's daily phone communication with me I reminded him of the commitment he had made with me that:- "Your position was to put together all the necessary documentation, which will be required to transfer the funds to an account, which will be nominated by me. By this I mean that the rights and privileges bestowed on the investor will be transferred to you. You further assured me that all legalities will be dealt with by you and I would not be at any financial risk as all the risk is on your side."

After reminding Bhathia of his commitment to me, he communicated the following day by phone, "I feel there may have to be a revision on the expenses retainer Because of the tax burden which comes to approximately $220,000 which I had to pay. I was able to secure a loan of $185,000 that was the only equity left on my house. I also had to make arrangements to secure the balance of $35,000 through a close friend in China. That is why Donald you must pay the Lawyer the €16.000 sixteen Thousand Euros which is a small amount to pay compare to what you will be gaining.

By the time the conversation ended I was in a state of utter confusion. "What do I do next?" I am not a drinking man, but I poured myself a Bourbon and thought about the whole situation for a while. I did not and could make a decision that day. I slept on it as the saying goes. The next day I communicated with Ms Elias the Lawyer. I told her that I was ready to transfer the €16.000 Euros to her bank in Belgium provided I received from her, proper identification details together with her Company's Registration Certificate for verification. I would also need the name of the Account Holder. In the meantime arrangements have been made with my Bank, "The Royal Bank of Scotland", to transfer the expenses retainer.

It was during this period that I informed the bank of the amount of money I was expecting from the inheritance. They told me that because of the current world situation and banking rules, they would not accept the funds without full details of the source together with proper documentation. At this stage the bank was expressing concerns about sending the €16.000 Sixteen Thousand Euros to an off-shore bank account in Belgium. The officer felt that the money should go to the Lawyers bank account in Singapore. The officer of RBS The Royal Bank of Scotland advised me to obtain from the recipient the name of the Account Holder as it was absent from her bank details. It was at this stage that I contacted

Ms Elias the Lawyer for further information. She became agitated and very aggressive; then she tells me that I should have requested this information earlier and she would have provided that information.

I told her that this information is a vital requirement for my own security and legal requirement of the bank before the money can be sent. I also need this information for my own and peace of mind. Miss Elias advised me to check the Singapore Law Society Directory for her Company's name. I looked on the Internet, but sadly Lee Associates BVBA was not listed. There was a <u>Lee Associates</u>, but they did not have any knowledge of Ms Michelle Elias.

Further discussions with Royal Bank of Scotland convinced me that it was unwise to send these funds to the account in Belgium. The red light at the back of my mind was now flashing faster and faster. I was in constant contact with my bank. I **must say here that the advice from the bank was priceless.** The officer advised me, that from his experience the whole affair looks like a fraud, and as a valued customer they would recommend that I do not to send the €16.00 sixteen thousand Euros. However he said if you wish to send the money the bank will follow your instructions, but be a where that the bank will not be held responsible for the loss of your funds.

Needless to say the solicitor Ms Elias did not send the requested documents. At this stage I had already signed the Power of Attorney for her to act, and verify the documents on my behalf at the so call Singapore Claim Board/FOB Foreign Operations Department. It was during this period that every one connected with the operation in Singapore including Bhathia Keok was notified of my intentions.

Within days I received a very angry phone communication from Bhathia telling me that as a banker he had to follow his client's instructions, therefore he sees no reason why the bank should follow my instructions. He was very, very angry, and would not listen to what I had to say. At this stage my mind was made up; not to send any money to the solicitor Ms Elias.

I was now ready to walk away from the whole affair when out of the blue Bhathia phone and apologise to me for his behaviour. He put his action down to his frustration. I was not in any mood to have a dialogue with him so I accepted his apologies and promised to send him a written communication the following day.

As promised I sent him a Fax explaining my reasons why I was not prepared to send the €16.000 sixteen thousand Euros to Ms Elias' bank in Belgium even though I had signed the **Power of Attorney**. He said to me., "If this is causing you a problem I will make arrangements to get the funds elsewhere in order to pay the Lawyer." I said "That is entirely up to you". I did not have to wait long for a response.

Several days later, I received another phone communication. He told me that he had found someone who would put up the €16.000 sixteen thousand Euros but in order for them to put up the funds they will need to have half of the Inheritance money. I told him that, this proposal was unacceptable and I could not see how he could even consider bringing such proposal to me at this stage. The conversation ended with him saying "I am only trying to help Donald." I told him I am considering travelling to Singapore to meet him, the Lawyer, and the rest of the party at the FOB. He suggested that, because I had an operation I could cancel the Power of Attorney I had signed with Lee Associates BVBA. He went on to say. "You could give your wife the Power of Attorney and then send her to verify the documents in Singapore with the Claim Board and the Foreign Operations Department. It would not cost you €16000 Euros". I also declined this proposal.

The pressure was coming from all quarters, I received a Fax communication from a Mr. Feng of the so called FOB (Foreign Operations Department, who advised me that I had only seven working days before the claim expired and the funds would, automatically, be retuned to the Bank. I responded to him immediately saying:- . "Further to our telephonic conversation of *Thursday 25 August 2004* regarding the above claim, I am surprised to be advised that Neither you nor Ms Elias, the Accredited Lawyer, did not inform me that there was a time limit on this claim. The Tax liability has been paid and the Tax Clearance Certificate is in your possession. All other documents are on the file. The only outstanding matter is the €16,000 (Euros) that the Lawyer requested for Registration Fee, IMR Form, Affirmation of Documents and Stamp Duty. This money is in my bank account ready to be transmitted to the Firm's Client Account provided the accredited Lawyer can verify her account details, on Official Headed Notepaper, together with Registration Certificate. Miss Elias had advised me to check the Singapore Law Society Directory for her Company's name. I checked on the Internet, but sadly that Law firm is not listed.

There is a <u>Lee Associates</u> whose Offices are at 111 Amoy Street, Singapore, but there is no relationship between them and Lee Associates BVBA and Miss Michelle Elias when I contacted them. "That is the problem at the moment I said" The Senior Auditor of the Royal Bank of Scotland tried to speak to you today on my behalf. I was advised that you hung the phone up on him. He was then unable to make further contact. I said he was only doing his job considering the volatile financial climate that exists it the world today.

Although my Doctor has recommended that I should not undertake any long haul travel, because of Chronic back pain I am still prepared to take the long journey to Singapore to verify the documents within Seven days if the problem continued with the lawyer. You mention that the funds will revert to the bank automatically. Naturally I expect that the Tax paid, will also, automatically revert to sender. In light of the above I would appreciate it if you will arrange a new date to enable me to make travel arrangements to come Singapore. I await your response.

As is my usual practice I informed Bhatia of the letter I had received from the FOB.I told him of my concerns, His reply was, "Don't worry all will be fine you'll see". I said "what do you mean". He said "there is no time limit on the Inheritance Claim once the Tax liability has been paid and the relevant documents filed". I accepted his explanation. Bhathia usually telephone me at around 8.50 A.M and right on "Q" the following day the phone rang it was the man himself when I answered the phone. We greeted each other politely; He said, "Donald I suggest you cancel the agreement with the lawyer

43

and give me the **Power of Attorney.** I would go to the Foreign Operations Deportment and verify the documents on your behalf. Because another person is involved, the inheritance money will have to be divided three ways Donald". Right at that moment, my mind was truly made up to travel to Singapore. I told him that I was coming to Singapore to meet him, the Lawyer, and the rest of the party at the [FOB] Foreign Operations Deportment to verify the documents myself. He replied "that is a very good idea; the whole operation would then be completed. Please send me your itinerary.

I informed the Bank Royal Bank of Scotland that I was planning to travel to Singapore to sort out the problem with the lawyer and verify the inheritance documents, I also told them that when I got to Singapore, if everything was in order I would communicate with them to transfer the funds. I made the travel arrangements then *on August 13, 2004,* Flight number; QF32 Depart from London Heathrow 15-August 2004 at12.15 PM >> Arrival at Singapore Changi Airport 16-August-16-2004 at 08.05 AM >> Accommodation: BERJAYA Hotel, 83 Duxton Road, Singapore, 089540 Telephone: (65)6227 7678 - Fax (65) 62271232

Bhathia confirmed receipt of the Itinerary and said he was looking forward to meeting me. He also said that if he was unable to me when I landed he would make the necessary arrangement for someone to meet me on his behalf., He went on to say that he would meet me at the hotel at 0900 AM Singapore time. That was the arrangement, everything was in place. The time had come, my mind was truly made up. I was going to Singapore to meet Bhathia and all his Associates.

Chapter: 7

The Journey Begins

On Sunday 15th. August 2004, when my wife and I took a taxi to London Heathrow Airport, Terminal 4. There was an extremely long queue at the check in. It seemed that the whole of London was travelling to Australia via Singapore. I was in considerable pain and feeling very poorly indeed. After waiting for over two hours, my wife spoke to a stewardess, telling her that I was in considerable pain and asked if she could do anything to help. The Stewardess was very kind and within 20 to 30 minutes she got me checked in and I was able to sit down. I took some pain-killers and tried to relax. The pain eased a bit, but I was still anxious about my journey into the unknown. However, before proceeding to the departure lounge I gave my wife a hug, and a kiss and waved goodbye. More than an hour had passed before we were asked to go to gate number xx for boarding. Although I had requested an Aisle seat, I was given a Window seat that was very uncomfortable. It was made even worse, when, after the meal was served, the passenger in the middle, an Asian gentleman, opened his case took out a litre bottle of Whisky, and drank the lot on his way to Singapore. Well, he slept the rest of the journey, but mostly on the German passenger in the aisle seat and me at the, throwing his arms around my neck, then on the German passenger. It seemed the drink had made him very affectionate and he thought we were his buddies. It was most uncomfortable and did little to ease my pain and anxiety.

On arriving at Singapore, I proceeded through immigration with the rest of the passengers, where I hand over my passport to the officer, I was asked the usual questions. What is the purpose of your visit?" I said "business". How long are you staying etc, etc. I answered appropriately. The officer stamped my Passport and issued me with a visa for the duration of my stay. I collected my luggage in the normal manner then continued through nothing to declare at Custom. I then proceeded to the main concourse to see if anyone was there to meet me. **"There was no one".** I went to the meeting point and asked the operator to make an announcement that the person meeting Mr. Lawson should come to the meeting point *"Again there was no one"* I waited a little over two (2) hours outside the exit gate, still there was no one to meet me. I then took a Taxi to the hotel which was booked for me by the travel agent. The journey to the Hotel, should have taken half an hour it took three quarters of an hour. The fare should have been around ($50) Fifty Singapore dollars, I was charged ($125) One Hundred & Twenty Five Singapore dollars. To my surprise, I discovered that I was in China Town.

After driving through the beautiful area of Singapore it was a culture shock for me. The hotel was equally distressing. I had booked a non-smoking room, but I got instead, one which was filthy, smelt of stale cigarette smoke and cockroaches in the bathroom. I called the Travel Agents who had made the booking. I told them that I did not wish to stay there because the place was filthy and in China Town. They could not do anything until the next day so I had to spend a night in this hotel. The following day I was booked into the Phoenix hotel. However, before leaving BERJAYA Hotel, at 83 Duxton Road, I telephoned Mr. Jagger of the FOB Foreign Operations Department.

The person at the other end of the line knew exactly who I was. He wanted to know at which hotel I was staying. I gave him the address and telephone number of the Hotel. He went on to tell me that my claim is fraudulent. There is another Lawson who has made a claim to the inheritance funds. I told him, what he was saying to me was incorrect as I was informed by Bhithia Keok that the Probate Office in Hong Kong had investigated the claim. There was no other claimant at the end of the investigation period. During the conversation he said that he would still have to contact the Singapore Fraud Department. I said, "please do so I will be waiting here for them."

Before leaving Hotel Berjaya I telephoned the Lawyer, Ms Elias for an appointment. She told me that she was busy in Court and could not see me until 11.15 am on. Thursday 18th August at the Centennial Tower address. I then checked out and left the hotel at 12.15 pm the same day Tuesday 17 August 2004. I then travel to the Phoenix Hotel that was booked for me by the travel agent and checked in. Before leaving Hotel Berjaya, I left a instructions at the Reception that, if Bhathia or the Police turned up I could be found at the Phoenix Hotel. After settling down at the Phoenix with a snack, I tried several times to make contact with Bhathia without success. It was the satellite number, which was very expensive to say the least. I was now Jet lagged and in severe pain. I laid across the bed and fell asleep. I woke up some (3) three hours later. I unpacked my luggage, had a shower and got dressed.

It was bright and sunny outside. I decided to take a walk to familiarise myself with the area.

Returning from my walk several hours later I went for dinner in the Hotel restaurant around 7.30 pm. It was very strange dining alone in a foreign Country. I did not feel much like conversation anyway. I was very disappointed and extremely anxious, that the people who had promised to meet me were nowhere to be found. I felt like the proverbial "Fish out of Water"

After dinner I went back into the lobby and the Porter who handled my luggage earlier that afternoon, chatted with me for about 15 to 20 minutes. During our conversation he asked me if I wanted tip. (meaning friendly advice) I said "yes if it is a good tip". He advised me, that in order to save money it would be cheaper to eat outside. I can also buy some groceries like tea, biscuits, coffee and milk, take it back to my hotel room. I could have it whenever I want. I thanked him for his kind advice and said "see you tomorrow all being well". I went back to my suite and watched TV till late. >>

The Appointments

The following morning August 18 -2004 there was still no news from Bhathia or any one else so I had my I shower, dressed and went down for breakfast. After breakfast I made several telephone calls to Bhathia without success. I was truly worried, but I was slowly coming to terms with the fact that this was a major scam by Bhathia and his Associates. However, I was not going to close the chapter just yet. I had an appointment to keep with the lawyer Miss Elias .

At about 10.30 AM Thursday 18th August 2004 I went to the venue to keep the appointment with Miss Elias the Lawyer at the Centennial Tower, a short journey from the Phoenix Hotel. Before leaving the Phoenix, I left a message with the hotel phone operator that, if Bhathia called he was to tell him that I have gone to a meeting with Miss Elias the Lawyer, and would contact him on my return.

When I reached the Centenntel Tower "a massive building". I went to the reception and inquired for Lee Associates BVBA, The attendant made a thorough check. "I am afraid there is no Law Firm of that name here Sir" "However there is a Law firm with the name LEE & LEE on the 18th floor. Are you sure this is not the firm you want?" I said "no it is not". His said finally. "Sorry I couldn't help you." I was now well and truly depressed. I left the building. I went for a walk around the area to clear my head, and to see if I could find some answers. None came to mind. I caught a taxi from the taxi bay and retuned to the Phoenix Hotel. I inquired at the reception if there were any messages, for me. ***"There was none"***

Donald S. Lawson

I was still in a lot of pain, so I took some pain relief tablets and skipped lunch. After an hour or two I telephoned the Singapore number of the Lawyer. The same original voice mail answered saying,"Law Offices, If you wish to speak to a *legal practitioner*, press 1, if you wish to send a fax press 2. I pressed 1 and a voice came on the phone, and repeated "Law Offices". I told the person at the end of the line that I went to the Centennial Tower to keep my appointment with Ms Elias who was unavailable, and that there was no Law Firm with the name Lee Associates BVBA at the address given. At that moment the phone went dead, I tried to phone the number again but all I got was a disconnection tone there was no further contact with Ms. Elias the so called accredited Lawyer.

Now I was running out of options so I decided to contact the Law Firm Lee & Lee who had an Office at the Centennial Tower. Lee Kuan Yew is one of the co- founders of Lee & Lee, He was also the former Prime Minister of Singapore. Lee & Lee is one of the largest and leading law firms in Singapore, providing a comprehensive range of legal services for the differing needs of individuals and companies in the area and further a-field. That is why I chose to speak to one of their Legal Representatives to get some advice as to what I could do.

I spoke to one Miss Yew and told her the full story of the inheritance claim, and why I was in Singapore. She told me that I was not the first person to make contact with the firm Lee & Lee regarding this sort of claim mostly from the United Kingdom. She went on to say that their Law firm have spent thousand of Singapore dollars advising people against these fraudsters who are not residents of Singapore. She went on to say that this is clearly a scam, and the only advised she could give at this time, is that I report the whole matter to the local police in Singapore.

Before the conversation ended she told me that she was in sympathy with my problems, and if there was any further developments I should not hesitate to contact her. "I thank her for the advice and the conversation ended". I was truly unhappy and distressed to say the least. Later that day Thursday 18th August 2004 I telephoned my wife in London. I told her the full story what had happened, and asked her if she could send Bhatia a Fax on my behalf:

This is what she wrote on *August 20, 2004* :> Hello Bhathia

I am distressed and concerned that my husband is now in Singapore and you have not bothered to make the effort to see him. Despite the many telephone calls he made to you. You have done nothing. It does not make any sense. What would have happened if I had come to Singapore on my husband's behalf as you had suggested?. You would not meet me, your son would not meet me and I would be stranded in this strange land. You are always calling my husband friend, What sort of a friend are you?. As I understand it, Friends are people one can trust. My husband is unwell, as you know, and despite Doctor's advice he made the trip because he trusted you, and you assured him, that you would meet up with him in Singapore. He is very distressed and this trip has cost over £2000 to date. How could you do this to the man you call your friend? I am sure you will be able to find someone to read This fax letter for you, as I know many of your colleagues speak perfect English. If there is any humanity left in you please get in touch with my husband. Do the right thing Mr. Bhatia. Mrs. Lawson.

I was desperate to speak to this man so on Friday 20ᵗʰ August 2004 I tried again to make contact by phone to him, to my surprise he answered the phone and immediately started shouting and accusing me of coming to Singapore to take all the Inheritance money without giving him anything. My reaction to this neurotic outburst was surprise and disbelief. I said to him you invited me to come to Singapore, if that was my intention, why would I send you my Itinerary and you agreeing to meet me at the Airport and the Hotel?" He was still carrying on shouting that it was his money and that he had another Mr. Lawson who would be replacing me and putting up the money for the legal fees. I was flabbergasted to say the least It had become very clear to me that this was a full blown scam, as was told to me by my Bank, Royal Bank of Scotland, the Law Firm Lee & Lee and many others.

However, at about 2.30 pm the same Friday I took a taxi from the Phoenix Hotel towards the East Coast where the so-called (FOB) Foreign Operations Department is supposed to be located. The taxi driver told me that from his knowledge there is no such place. This is a residential area and no business for the bank of China would be conducted in this area of Singapore. Even though I knew the journey was a fruitless one I did not turn back. I just wanted to see more of the area for my self. Every one was right the East Cost was not a business area, it was a residential area.

On my way back to the Phoenix Hotel, I knew I that I could not leave the matter the way it was. I decided that I was going to inform the Bank of China and the Singapore Fraud Police about the whole Inheritance Plot that Bhathia and his Associates had devised. Because I was in a foreign Land and all alone I was not sure if I should report the matter to the Authorities in Singapore, or wait until I was back in the United Kingdom. Like A flash of inspiration my mind was made up, I decided to wait until my return to the United Kingdom before making a formal report to the Authorities. Back at the Hotel I had built up a relationship with one of the Concierge attendant whose name was Lee Feng. I told him that I went to the East Coast to find the so called Foreign Operations Department that represent the Bank of China. There was no such place, "It is al residential" He looked at me with a smirk on his face, then he said "you could have save yourself the taxi fair if you had listen to me when I told you that the East Coast was not a business area". We are now on first name basis, so he said to me "Donald you been had like a lot of people before you. all you have to do for the rest of your stay is to enjoy the beautiful scenery of Singapore".

I replied that I would just do that. It is a brilliant idea. We chatted for another ten to fifteen minutes then I left, went up to my room and made myself a cup of tea. I watched some television and tried to relax to ease the pain. For several hours the whole operation was still going round and round in my head. It was difficult to relax but I did manage to have cat nap.

After my cat nap I went for dinner outside of the hotel. After dinner, as usual with nothing much to do I went back to my room and telephoned my wife. I told her all that was happening, pouring out all my disappointment to get some moral support. "She did give me a lot of moral support. She was my tower of strength that was really needed. I watched television until late into the night. The past week was a total disaster and I was not going to have my first weekend in Singapore ruined. I slept until .approximately11a.m or there about. I had my shower, got dressed and made myself a lovely cup of coffee. This had become my normal routine.

There was a lot of activity in the hotel, guests checking in and out; it was more so than normal, because it was the weekend. It was the same everywhere the shopping centre, and the restaurants. For the first time since landing in Singapore I felt so relaxed that I wanted to capture the scenery. I went and bought myself a Panasonic Video Camera. I also shopped for presents for my dear wife and friends. Every one in the shop desperately trying to sell their wares. One has to be strong and not a shopperholic.. However, I did buy some lovely presents including some lovely Pearl necklace for my special friend my wife. It was a very hot and sticky day and the only place I needed to be is back at the air conditioned hotel with my shopping.

It was about three (3) pm when I arrived back at the hotel I got into the lift to the Eight (8th.) floor. I entered my room and threw all the shopping on the other bed as this was a double room. I was tired and in a lot of pain, I took some painkillers and in no time, I was a sleep. I did'nt wake up until about 8.30 pm, I decided to skip dinner and break the routine. Instead of having a one man meal I ordered a lobster sandwich meal from the room service menu at around 10.30. Pm. It was very nice, then I settled down to watch a Singapore documentary which was very educational; and finally the BBC world news.

ll retire to bed, but I could not sleep. Every time I fell asleep I was awakened by the guests and there friends in the adjoining room., The noise nuisance continued until around four-thirty (4-30) am Singapore time. I finally went to sleep.

After waking up later that Sunday morning I entered into the normal routine did my Stretching exercises, shaved, showered, got dressed. Had a cup of coffee, and watched some local and international news. I did not feel much for anything to eat after I had finished my routine. it is now too late for breakfast. I had woken up a bit late and had missed breakfast anyway. I decided to go on a sightseeing bus tour. Whilst in the lobby I went to reception and advised them of the excessive noise nuisance that had kept me awake until around four (4) AM. The receptionist apologised and asked me to report any such further behaviour and they will take immediate steps to ensure good behaviour. They offered me a small reduction on my bill as a gesture of goodwill, which I accepted.

I then left the reception had a diet coke and a tuna sandwich in the cafeteria. I got on to one of the sightseeing bus which toured the city and some outskirts. The tour lasted more than two (2) hours, and guess what, I had a new video camera locked away in my security box in my hotel room. It was too late to go back for it. Although I did not have the video camera with me the good memories of the beautiful sites will always remain with me. On returning from the tour, I had something to eat at one of the local café/restaurants. The food was lovely and because I was hungry, it tasted even better than it looked. Whilst I was having a lovely meal, I noticed it was dark outside. About ten to fifteen minutes later the havens opened up, the rain was coming down in buckets. I have never seen such large raindrops. It did not last very long but during the short period, I would guess that about two to three inches of rain fell. Half an hour later the sun was shining brightly again. The humidity was very high. One would hardly guess that half an hour previously, the rain was falling down in buckets.

I was not far away from the Phoenix hotel where I was staying; about twenty-five minutes walking distance, so I slowly walked the short distance back. I did not have much back pain that day thank goodness. Getting back to the hotel, I was sweating and sticky so I had myself a shower. Afterwards I had a Bourbon from the mini bar and watched some television programs. At no time that day did I think about Bhathia Keok the man who had invited me to come to Singapore to meet his Associates in order to verify the inheritance documents. I just continued watching television until about Ten (10) PM. I treated myself to the famous lobster sandwich meal from room service menu. I went to sleep around midnight. There was no loutish behaviour from the guests next door thank goodness. I slept till about Eight (8) AM Monday 21st August 2004.

Again I performed my normal routine stretching exercises shower, got dressed etc., then went for breakfast. After breakfast I went back to the room. I decided to try once more to make contact with Bhathia by phone and fax. I sat down and wrote this message on the Phoenix Hotel Note paper as follows:-

Dear Bhatia

You have invited me to Singapore to finalise matters. After travelling over 11,000 miles you did NOT send anyone to meet me. You did NOT attend any of the Appointments you made with me. I can only come to one conclusion. Your Word is not Your Bond. My Word is my Bond.

I sincerely hope you will come and see me at the Hotel above before my Departure on Monday 23rd August 2004. I hope you will make the effort to see me before the matter becomes un-solve-able.

Video Diary Transcript.
After sending the Fax I decided to do a Video Diary.

Hello Curlah, I am here alone in this hotel room very distressed and in a lot of pain. Since I came here, I have not seen or heard from Bhatia who has invited me to come here. I have not heard from Ms Ellis Elias of Lee Associates BVBA the so called Accredited Lawyer approved by the Singapore Claim Board. Mr Jagger and Finna of the so called Foreign Operations Department have also disappeared. I shall be leaving here by Wednesday 23rd August 2004 and all I can tell you is that I HAVE BEEN HAD by a bunch of con-men. However, I could have lost a lot more if it was not. Thanks to the Royal Bank of Scotland. **End of transcript**

Needless to say that there was no response to the telefax communication from Bhathia and there was no phone connection to his conspirators. Everyone was keeping a low profile, except the real Lawyer Miss Yew of LEE & LEE who's office was at Centennial Tower. I told her that I was leaving for the United Kingdom on Wednesday 23rd August 2004 She wished me luck and urged me again to report the whole episode to the Singapore fraud Police. I replied "you can rest assured that I will". Conversation ended.

End of the Journey

Finally on Tuesday 22- 08-2004, the day before my departure, my morning routine started as it has been since my arrival at the Phoenix hotel. This time I did not miss my breakfast. After breakfast I got into a taxi and headed for China Town. I wanted to see if I was correct about this area. Nothing had changed, except that in front of many shops bundles of incense sticks were burning. The air was thick with the smell of burning incense. Other shops were being washed and scrubbed by owners or their staff, with buckets and brushes. They were on hands and knees. As I have said earlier this is a completely different setting from elsewhere that I have seen in Singapore. I walked around the area for about an hour then took a taxi from the Taxi Bay and returned to the Hotel. Back at the Hotel, I completed my packing. As this was my final day I could not resist going to the Café/restaurant where I had a delicious Lobster Sandwich with a cold drink. I told one of the Restaurant staff with whom I had become quite friendly, that I was leaving the next day. He wished me a safe journey and hoped that I would come back to Singapore in the not too distant future.

After leaving the restaurant I walked around the shops to see if there was anything I had forgotten. I didn't see anything that

I really wanted. I had everything that I needed. As I walked back to the hotel a sad feeling came over me as I thought of Bhathia and how he had completely deceived me with his lies and false representations by his colleagues. I stopped for a brief while by the park and watched the waterfalls and lovely trees. My only reward was the kindness of the few people with whom I spoke and the beautiful scenery which was truly magical. This I will never forget. I got back to the hotel at about 6.00pm,and relaxed with a cup of tea. I telephoned home to confirm that I would be leaving Singapore on the evening of the 23rd August. I watched television for a while and went to bed at around 9.00pm.

Singapore Departure

Wednesday 23rd August is the date of my departure. I woke early that morning, had breakfast, but felt very uneasy in my stomach. I spoke with the Concierge telling him that I would be leaving today for London. He wished me a safe journey and said that he was sorry that I had traveled all this way and did not achieve anything. I then went to Reception and asked if I could remain in the room until 2.00pm as my flight would be leaving very late that day. They were very kind and said I could remain until 2.00pm. I checked out at 2.00 pm as agreed.

The Porter outside the hotel hailed a taxi for me; I got in and asked the driver to take me to Changi Airport. The driver was pleasant and talkative. We chatted about this and that, small talk really. Then unexpectedly he asked. "Was your trip to Singapore successful?" I was a bit surprised but replied,

"Not really." He replied, "I am sorry to hear this." At that stage of the Journey, I requested him to drive along the East Cost Road. This is where the so-called Claim Board and Foreign Operations Department are supposed to have been located. There was no such place, so we continued our journey to the airport. The fare to the airport was Sixty (60) Singapore Dollars. There is a massive difference to the fare I paid when I arrived in Singapore the fare then was over One Hundred & Forty (140) Singapore dollars.

I paid the driver $70.00 for the journey, which includes tip. I got myself a trolley for my luggage, looked around the concourse for a while and then checked in my luggage. I then went through emigration. I telephoned my wife. When she answered the phone, she told me that she had telephoned the Hotel and was told that I had already left. We chatted for a few minutes, and then I reminded her of the arrival times of travel and told her that I would phone when I arrived in Frankfurt. I then went to get some Duty Free shopping. After the shopping, I went for a snack in one the cafeterias. Whilst having my snack I heard an announcement over the Loudspeaker, "Would Mr Donald Lawson report to emigration." My stomach did a double turn and I sat there terrified. I did not attempt to report to emigration, but sat rigid in my seat. The announcement was made two more times but the third time the announcer said "Mr Donald Lawson holding an Australian Passport, please report to emigration immediately."

I breathed a great sigh of relief and my heart started beating normally again. I finally took up my seat in the Departure lounge for the long wait before my departure from Singapore to London Heathrow via. Frankfurt. Under normal circumstances

I would start a conversation, but on this occasion I was not able to do so. I sat in the Departure lounge full of people of all nationalities feeling alone and extremely vulnerable watching the time slowly ticking way. I wondered how I could have allowed myself to get into this state. I wanted to cry but anger got in the way together with sadness and the extreme desire to get on the plane. Finally, at about 8.30pm local time the announcement came to proceed to the gate for departure to London via Frankfurt. I was overjoyed to be leaving Singapore. We all boarded the Airliner. I was fortunate to get an aisle seat, much, better than the one I had on the journey to Singapore When the plane taxied along the run way for take off and the wheels were off the ground I was truly relieved to be leaving Singapore.

For the first time during those seven days, I was really, really, happy to be coming home. Indeed, I was on top of the world finally on my way home. After dinner, I enjoyed some in flight entertainment and then went to sleep. I did not check on the time. From what I recall the flight from Singapore to Frankfurt was pleasant. At about 8.00 o'clock European time we landed at Frankfurt Airport where, we were to get a connection to Heathrow. Alas, that was not to be. I telephoned my wife from Frankfurt Airport telling her of the change of travel plans.

After a long wait at Frankfurt Airport, myself and other Heathrow passengers were told that the flight to Heathrow was cancelled, and that we would be re-directed to London City Airport, and then by Coach to Heathrow. When we got to London City Airport, I felt like kissing the ground but refrained from doing so in case my fellow traveller thought I was crazy, or intoxicated with the beauty and wonders of Singapore. The wait for a Coach was extremely long and many passengers chose not to wait. En-route to Heathrow I decided that as I was passing my home I would get a taxi at a point near my home. The driver was very polite and agreed to set me down at a central point where I took a Taxi home. I telephoned my wife again and told her about this new plan. She was o.k. with this plan and said how much she had that she had missed me. I said "ditto". When I arrived home I was over the moon,I was trilled to be home, my wife greeted me with big hug and a kiss, we chatted for nearly an hour, then we had a lovely meal and couple glasses of Champagne. I spent the rest of the afternoon telling my wife about my adventure. I was getting very tired and exhausted due to the long flight; so I went to sleep for almost twelve hours, to the next day and into the weekend. >>>>>>>>

Chapter: 9

The Authorities

After settling down that day which was Friday 25 August 2004 I distributed the presents I bought to my family and friends every one was happy to see that I had arrived safely back in the United Kingdom . For the first time I felt safe I was on solid ground as the saying goes, I was ready to prepare for the next chapter in the Inheritance Scam with the Authorities. It had become clear to me whilst I was in Singapore that I was the victim of an elaborate Inheritance fraud by a bunch of sophisticated con artist and actors whose sole purpose is to extract solid cash from those who will fall into their con trap. I am lucky. I am the one that got away, and I owe it all to the Royal Bank of Scotland if it were not for the diligence of their Officers, I would have lost €16.000. Sixteen Thousand Euros. Instead my total cost for this experience is £3500 Three Thousand Five Hundred pounds I have no regrets. The cost of knowledge is priceless. I have travelled over 22 000 twenty two thousand air miles round trip to discover that there was no Inheritance money from a long lost deceased relative.. I have made a pledge to others and myself that I would inform the Bank of China, and the Singapore Fraud Police about this Inheritance Fraud that Bhathia Keok with others had instigated.

Over that weekend I lookup up the Telephone and Telefax numbers for Bank of China Singapore Branch. I telephone the bank and was told to send the information in writing to Mr. Feng. The following day I wrote:, Further to a telephonic conversation I had with one of your colleagues on Thursday 25 August 2004,. I received a letter from a person who describes himself as BHATHIA Keok Head of Internal Audit Department

(See attached Letter) I would be grateful if you could investigate this person, as I believe there is a syndicate of people representing themselves, as being connected to the Bank of China Singapore Branch There is at least one Judge, accredited Lawyer and others purporting to be Officers of the Singapore Claim Board, and the Foreign Operations Department of the Bank. I have in my possession, Passport details and other documents, which I will provide for your use. I wait to hear further from you in due course.

On the 21 August 2004 I sent the subject letters and all other relevant documents to Hu Bing Deputy Head of the Administration Department. I also went to my local Police Station in London to report the matter. I did not get much help. There is very little they could do in the United Kingdom. They said that It was up to the Hong Kong and Singapore Authorities to take action.

Then on the 27 August 2004, I received a positive response from Hu Bing of the Bank of China thanking me for bringing the matter to their attention. They also confirmed that the Bank of China Singapore branch did not issue the letter which Bhathia sent to me., They also confirmed that they were aware of the matter, which they believe to be an attempted fraud, and that they have reported the matter to the relevant Authority in Singapore. I also received communication from Christine Kua, Head of Human Resource Department from the Bank of China Singapore, informing me that I was not the only person who had received these letters and other documents from the subject. They, The Bank have been receiving letters with similar contents from various addressees since February 2004. Again, she confirms that they have reported the matter to the relevant Authority in Singapore. I was hopeful that at last something was about to happen. My spirit was lifted to new heights for the first time I believe that something positive was happening.

Donald S. Lawson

27 August 2004

Ref: AD/S58/2004

Donald S Lawson
21 Harvey House
Green Dragon Lane
Brentford TW8 0DH
Fax: 44 208 5801925

Dear Mr Lawson

Thank you for bringing our attention to the matter and for your fax of 25 August 2004, including the copy of letter from Bhathia Keok.

We confirm that the Bank of China, Singapore Branch did not issue the letter. We are aware of the matter which we believe is an attempted fraud and have reported to the relevant Authority in Singapore.

Your sincerely
For and on behalf of
Bank of China, Singapore

Hu Bing
Deputy Head
Administration Department

Bank of China Letter
One

66

中国银行 新加坡分行
BANK OF CHINA   SINGAPORE BRANCH

31 August 2004   BY FAX

Mr Donald S Lawson
Harvey House 21,
Green Dragon Lane
Brentford Middlesex
TW8 0DH
Fax : 44 208 5801925

Dear Mr Lawson

We refer to your fax of 30/8/2004.

We would like to let you know that you are not the only person who has received the letters plus documents from Bhathia Keok, we have been receiving letters with similar contents from various addressees since February this year.

Judging from the content of these letters, it is obvious that this is an attempted fraud. Thus we have reported the mater to the relevant authority who has advised you to lodge a local police report.

Yours sincerely
For and on behalf of
Bank of China, Singapore

Christine Kua
Head
Human Resource Department

4 Battery Road   Tel : (65) 65353611
Bank of China Building Fax : (65) 65343401
Singapore 049908   Telex : RS 23046 BKCHINA

Bank of China Letter
Two

I was hoping that the letters received from the Bank of China would shed some light on Bhathia Keoh who claimed he is the Head of Internal Audit Department to the Bank of China Singapore Branch. I was not surprised about this revelation in the above letters, I had known before my approach to the Bank of China that my dealing with the subject and his associates was a mistake, and I wanted more than anything to. Stop the subject pursuing further. Fraudulent activities. I was now ready to co-operate with the Singapore Fraud Department. I had no choice but wait, as the matter had been reported to the relevant Authority in Singapore by the bank. It was not long after communicating with the Bank of China Singapore Branch, that I receive a fax communication from a Shirley Chen, INSP Senor Investigation Officer, General Fraud Branch, and Commercial Affairs Department. She was referring to the letters I send to the Bank of China Singapore Branch regarding the subject Bhathia Keok ..She said matter was receiving their attention., She also request further information., This information was duly sent.

Our Ref: 0799-96(CFP)

Tel: (65) 65573748
Fax: (65) 62233171

Date: 10.09.2004

Mr Donald S Lawson
Harvey House 21
Green Dragon Lane
Brentford Middlesex
TW8 0DH

Fax: 44 208 5801925
Tel: 44 208 5687905

Dear Sir,

SUBJECT: BHATHIA KEOK

      Please refer to your letters to the Bank of China, Singapore, concerning the above-mentioned subject. The matter is receiving our attention.

2   I would appreciate if you fill me in on the details of the case:
        a) How did you get to know about the matter, e.g. via email, facsimile?
        b) How long have you been corresponding with Bhathia Keok and by which means, eg via telecommunications, email, facsimile? Kindly provide the contact numbers or email addresses.
        c) Were you asked to correspond with anyone else beside Bhathia Keok? Kindly provide their particulars and contact numbers if any.
        d) Have you remitted any money to Bhathia Keok? If so, kindly provide the details of the remittance, eg amount, mode of remittance(T.T / Bank Transfer), designated country, name of the recipient.
        e) Any other matters.

3   Should you have any queries, I could be contacted via Phone: (65) 65573748 or via email: shirley_chen@spf.gov.sg.

4   Regards.

Yours faithfully,

SHIRLEY CHEN, INSP
SENIOR INVESTIGATION OFFICER
GENERAL FRAUD BRANCH
COMMERCIAL AFFAIRS DEPARTMENT

COMMERCIAL AFFAIRS DEPARTMENT · SINGAPORE POLICE FORCE · MINISTRY OF HOME AFFAIRS
POLICE CANTONMENT COMPLEX. BLOCK D #06-70'. 391 NEW BRIDGE ROAD SINGAPORE 088783
TEL: 63260000   FAX: 62268472

FRAUD POLICE LETTER

During the months that followed I had several phone and fax communication with the Inspector to see how the investigation was progressing. I also sent all the relevant telephone and fax numbers, that Bhathia Keok and his colleagues were using to communicate. with me from 15th April 2004 to 17th August 2004.

Andrew Chung - Singapore Claim Board Telefax: 568279062
Albert Jagger. - Foreign Operations Department:
Telephone: 6562995507   Telefax: 6564151446
Michelle C Elias ,Telephone: 6563960725
Company Name:-Lee Associates BVBA Telefax: 6562995507
Bhathia Keok, Telephone: 0088 216466 55522
Telefax: 6564151446
Bhathia's son's Telephone: 6562995507 Singapore. From my observation Bhatia's son and Albert Jagger is the same. As well as this Telephone: 0088 216466 55522

I believe one Mr. Syria is the owner of this satellite phone number which is, Bhathia's contact number. Most of these telephone numbers are based in Singapore and not in Hong Kong. I have reason to believe that this group was operating around the East Cost of Singapore which is a residential area.

The inspector indicated to me during one of our conversations that these people are not residents of Singapore. It is hard to believe though that, the Police and all the facilities at their disposal, it would not be difficult for them to apprehend these bunch of con-artists. I can only tell you that either by lack of interest, or by design no one from the of Bank of China Singapore Branch, nor the Inspector, Senior, Investigation

Officer, General Fraud Branch, and Commercial Affairs Department have indicated to me, to date, the result of their investigations. I can only conclude that they have not been able to apprehend one single person from this Fraudulent group.

Despite this extra-ordinary experience, I have to give thanks to my wife and those other kind friends who have supported me during my ordeal; but most of all the Royal Bank of Scotland. Without their keen eyes and expertise, I would have lost well over Sixteen Thousand Euros, €16, 000. I am truly grateful to the Royal Bank of Scotland . At the end of all this there was no inheritance money to my knowledge. If there was , I did not receive it someone else has I can only tell you that the bunch of con-artists are still at large . I can also say, that despite all I have encountered, on Reflection I have learnt a great deal from this experience. i.e. wisdom, knowledge and above all a positive purpose for the greater good. I also come to understand and learn about the good people of Singapore who are not con men and or plotters.

The Singapore People
Following my brief visit to Singapore, It has come to my knowledge, that Singapore's geographical position and commercial success were major influences on the composition of its population. After it was founded by Sir Stamford Raffles, this small sea town was quickly established as a flourishing trading post. It became a magnet for migrants and merchants from China, the Indian subcontinent, and else where in the Middle East.

71

Singapore's different races live in perfect harmony together. They came in search of a better place to settle down, lured by the riches of the land and bringing with them their own cultures, languages, customs and festivals. Through intermarriage and integration, these diverse human ingredients' have merged into the multifaceted society that is unique to Singapore: a young nation with a vibrant diversities and cultural inheritance that is improving to this very day.

Singapore has a resident population of about 3.5 million, with a median age of 32 years. Between 1994 and 1996, population growth was 1.9 per cent. In terms of population by age, 22.8 per cent are 14 and below, 67.2 per cent are between 15 to 59, and 10 per cent are 60 and above. With population density of 4,702 persons per sq km, it is a crowded place to live in.

The Ethnic Groupings

The people of Singapore are a mixed bunch. Almost (77.3 per cent) are Chinese. The Malays make up 14.1 per cent, the Indians 7.3 per cent and others 1.3 per cent. Despite these neat categories, guessing someone's ethnic origins can be a challenge. The early immigrant history are a fair amount of intermarriages this have helped to create a mixed people attuned to the influence of different cultures. Don't be surprised if you meet people of Dutch or Portuguese descent, or Chinese with Muslim names, or mixed race Indians who speak fluent Mandarin--these are part of the elements that make Singapore a multiracial city.

Singapore Culture and Religions

Singapore is a cosmopolitan society where people live harmoniously and interaction among different races are commonly seen. The pattern of Singapore stems from the inherent cultural diversity of the island. The immigrants of the past have given the place a mixture of languages Chinese, Indian, and European, all of which have intermingled.

Behind the face of a modern city, these different races are still evident. The areas for the different races, which were designated to them by Sir Stamford Raffles, still remain although the bulk of Singaporeans do think of themselves as Singaporeans, regardless of race or culture. Each still bears its own special character.

The old streets of Chinatown can still be seen, "the Muslim characteristics are still conspicuous in Arab Street" the Little India along Serangoon Road still has its distinct ambience. Furthermore, there are marks of the British colonial influence in the Neo-Classical buildings all around the city. Each racial group has its own distinctive religion and there are colourful festivals of special significance all year round. Although the festivals are special to certain races, it is, nonetheless, enjoyed by all.

In Singapore, food is also readily and widely available. There are lots of cuisines to offer. They have, Chinese, Indian, Malay, Indonesian, Western and, Italian, Peranakan, Spanish, French, Thai and even Fusion. It is very common to savour other cultures' food and, Some of the food can be very intriguing. Indian food is relatively spicier, whereas Chinese food is less spicy and the Chinese enjoy seafood. Malay cooking uses coconut milk as their main ingredient. That makes their food very tasty, and highly recommended food outlets in Singapore.

Religious tolerance is essential in Singapore. In fact, religions often cross racial boundaries and some even merge in unusual ways in this modern country. Younger Singaporeans tend to combine a little of the mysteries of the older generation with the realistic world that they know of today. Religion is still an integral part of the cosmopolitan Singapore. Many of its most interesting buildings are religious, be it old temples, modern churches, or exotic mosques. An understanding of these buildings do play a part in contributing to the appreciation of their art.

Chinese Temples
Taoism, Confucianism, Buddhism, and ancestral worship are combined into a versatile mix in Chinese temples. Followers of the Tao (The Way) adhere to the teachings of the ancient Chinese legend, Lao Tzu. They are concerned with the balance of the Yin and Yang, which are opposite forces of heaven and earth, male and female. Feng Shui, literally translated as wind and water, also originated from Yin and Yang.

Ancestral worship is a common practice and the spirits of the dead, like the gods themselves, are temped with offerings. Most Buddhists are of the Mahayana school although there are some from the Theravada school. In Singapore, the Buddhist faith is linked with Taoism and the practical doctrine of Confucianism.

One will be able to find Christian churches of all denominations in Singapore. They were actually established with the arrival of various missionaries after the coming of Sir Stamford Raffles. Together with Buddhism, Islam, and Hinduism, Christianity is considered one of the four main religions today. There is quite a large number of Christians on the island. Minority faiths are not forgotten. There are at least two synagogues for the Jews and Sikhs. The Zoroastrians and Jains are also represented in Singapore.

The four official languages of Singapore are Mandarin, Malay, Tamil and English. English is the most common language used and is the language which unites the different ethnic groups. Children are taught in English at school but also learn their mother tongue to make sure they do not lose contact with their traditions.

Expatriates and foreigners may encounter language problems in the beginning of their stay in Singapore as many Singaporeans use Singlish to communicate. Singlish is a mix of English with other languages mixed into the English, sometimes phrases can end with funny terms like 'lah', 'leh', mah'. Chinese commonly use their own dialects to communicate, and sometimes, inter-dialect groups don't understand one another's language, as the language is vastly different. Except for Hokkien and Teochew, which have a closer link. The Malays use the language among their fellow races and the Indians speak Tamil. But whatever the race or religion, the country's community unite as one nation, where most religious or racial gaps are being bridged.

Singapore English has its origins in the schools of colonial Singapore. In the nineteenth century very few children went to school at all, and even fewer were educated in English. The people who spoke English and sent their children to English medium schools were mainly the Europeans. The Eurasians (people of mixed racial ancestry), some of the small minorities, such as the Jews, some of the Indians and Ceylonese, and also a group of Chinese people usually called the Straits Chinese, who had ancestors of long residence in the region, and who spoke a variety of Malay usually called Baba Malay which was influenced by Hokkien Chinese and by Bazaar Malay.

The fact that all these children would have known Malay probably explains why most of the loan words in Singapore Colloquial English are from Malay. The largest group of teachers were Eurasians, and there were also many teachers from Ceylon and India. European teachers were never more than a quarter of the total teaching staff in a school, and they usually taught the senior classes. These Europeans may have been from Britain (which at that time included Ireland) but were also from the USA, Belgium and France. The children in these schools would have been exposed to many varieties of English.

In the first twenty years of the twentieth century, English medium education became popular for all groups. Girls started going to school in larger numbers too. By the 1950s nearly all children went to school, and the majority were educated in English. By the 1980s. all education was in the medium of English (with children learning another language alongside English).

Singapore English grew out of the English of the playground of these children of various linguistic backgrounds who were learning English at school. As more and more of its people experienced learning English at school, English became widely spoken, alongside Singapore's many other languages. Since

Singapore became an independent Republic in 1965, the use of English has increased still further. For many Singaporeans, English is the main language. Many families speak English at home and it is one of the first languages learnt by about half of the current pre-school children.

Nearly everyone in Singapore speaks more than one language, with many people speaking three or four. Most children grow up bilingual from infancy and learn more languages as they grow up. Naturally the presence of other languages (especially various varieties of Malay and of Chinese) has influenced the English of Singapore. The influence is especially apparent in the kind of English that is used informally, which is popularly called Singlish. Singlish is a badge of identity for many Singaporeans.

Singapore English usually come from other languages spoken in Singapore, especially Malay and Hokkien. Speakers of Singlish are not necessarily aware of which language they are from however.

In conclusion I would emphasise that Singapore is a beautiful and clean country, and, although the book is entitled "The Singapore Plotters" , I would like to stress that it is a true story of what actually happened, and does not in any way reflect on the very good, kind and help Singaporeans, with whom I came into contact. Based upon my unfortunate experience, I can truly declare that a handful of rotten apples do not soil the whole basket. "In this case even 4 or five rotten apples will not spoil the whole basket.

Donald S. Lawson

My Reflection:

Today has a purpose, every day has purpose, Pay attention to that purpose, and you'll uncover this day's many treasures. There is a reason why you have arrived at this point. On this day there is much to be learned, to be accomplished, to be experienced and to be lived. When your thoughts, your actions and your efforts consistently follow a clear and positive purpose, achievement is inevitable. Look deeply at the things you treasure most, and you will see that purpose. Purpose brings together all the seemingly unconnected parts of life. Purpose creates positive value out of the triumphs and the setbacks alike. With a clear sense of purpose, your vast and magnificent resources are put to use in the service of an even greater good. With a clear sense of purpose, even the tragedies and disappointments cannot stop you. There is always some part of you that knows what your purpose is right now. The more of your life you connect to that purpose, the more magnificent life will be in the end.

The End.
Ralph Marston"

About the Author

For a very long time it has been my dream to write a book, but I did not get around to doing so. I spent many years doing other things but the opportunity never presented itself. I feel, however this is the right time to put pen to paper as this book is the direct result of an episode in my life that I believe should be told. It is a real life experience although some may think it is stranger than fiction.

I have been involved in the Music Business with my own Music Publishing and Record Labels, Seven Sun and Calendar Records.

After leaving the Music Business, I spent some time as an investor and Consultant in the Financial Markets. No doubt, there are many stories to be told and this is one of many. I feel that I now have the time and materials to realise my dream. Over the years, I kept that dream alive, because I believed that the opportunity would present itself. I faced the challenges that kept that dream alive. I have come to the cornerstone of my dream and this is the beginning of that dream.

This is one of many episodes of a larger picture.